BFI FILM CLASSICS

. . . .

Edward Buscombe

SERIES EDITOR

Cinema is a fragile medium. Many of the great classic films of the past now exist, if at all, in damaged or incomplete prints. Concerned about the deterioration in the physical state of our film heritage, the National Film and Television Archive, a Division of the British Film Institute, has compiled a list of 360 key films in the history of the cinema. The long-term goal of the Archive is to build a collection of perfect show-prints of these films, which will then be screened, regularly at the Museum of the Moving Image in London in a year-round repertory.

B FI Publishing has now commissioned a series of books to stand alongside these titles. Authors, including film critics and scholars, film-makers, novelists, historians and those distinguished in the arts, have been invited to write on a film of their choice, drawn from the Archive's list. Each volume will present the author's own insights into the chosen film, together with a brief production history and a detailed filmography, notes and bibliography. The numerous illustrations have been specially made from the Archive's own prints.

With new titles published each year, the BFI Film Classics series is rapidly growing into an authoritative and highly readable guide to the great films of world cinema.

BLACKMAIL

·····················

Tom Ryall

BFI PUBLISHING

First published in 1993 by the
BRITISH FILM INSTITUTE
21 Stephen Street, London W1P 1PL

The British Film Institute exists
to encourage the development of film, television
and video in the United Kingdom,
and to promote knowledge, understanding and
enjoyment of the culture of the moving image.
Its activities include the National Film and
Television Archive; the National Film Theatre;
the Museum of the Moving Image;
the London Film Festival; the production and
distribution of film and video; funding and support for
regional activities; Library and Information Services;
Stills, Posters and Design; Research,
Publishing and Education; and the monthly
Sight and Sound magazine.

British Library Cataloguing-in-Publication Data
A catalogue record for this book is available from the British Library.

ISBN 0–85170–356–9

Designed by
Andrew Barron & Collis Clements Associates

Typesetting by
Fakenham Photosetting Limited, Norfolk

Printed in Great Britain by
The Trinity Press, Worcester

PN
1997
.B5776
R93
1993

CONTENTS

....

ACKNOWLEDGMENTS

I should like to acknowledge the general help and support of many friends and colleagues at Sheffield Hallam University and, especially, Van Gore, my Head of Division, and John Kirby and the staff of the School of Cultural Studies Library. Also crucial to the project were staff in the British Film Institute Library, the Stills, Posters and Designs Department and the National Film and Television Archive, and I am grateful to Edward Buscombe for helpful editorial comments on the initial draft. Markku Salmi checked the credits.

Alice (Anny Ondra) and the laughing jester

INTRODUCTION

....

Blackmail, made in 1929, seems quintessential Hitchcock. A blonde heroine, a dull policeman, a chase in and around a familiar public landmark, a killing, suspense, even a cameo performance by the director himself, together with a number of stylistic 'touches' readily ascribable to him. It was Hitchcock's tenth feature as director, yet only the second of his films to incorporate those features of the 'Hitchcockian' universe we now take for granted.

While *The Lodger*, made a few years earlier in 1926, also dealt with violence, passion and suspense, and was both a critical and commercial success, Hitchcock's other films of the 1920s are a medley of theatrical and literary adaptations. *Downhill*, *Easy Virtue* and *The Manxman* for example, draw on plays by Ivor Novello and Noël Coward and a Hall Caine novel, and suggest a conventional British film-maker translating the frothy West End stage and the middlebrow novel to the screen. *Blackmail* itself was based on a successful West End play but Hitchcock was to open it out and to inject into it a degree of cinematic panache, especially in some of the 'silent' sequences, which pushed well beyond the conventions of theatrical and literary adaptation. In addition, his exploitation of the new dimension of dialogue presented film critics and historians with a classic sequence – the 'knife' scene – which has been endlessly analysed as an exemplary use of sound.

Blackmail was released in June 1929. It was hailed as the 'first British all-talkie film',[1] although some commentators have drawn attention to British Lion's talkie, *The Clue of the New Pin*, released some months earlier in March 1929. However, the release of *Blackmail* inaugurated a history of critical commentary which began in the first serious English-language film journal, *Close Up*, in the same year and which still continues. In 1991, for instance, the British journal *Screen* published a lengthy analytical article on the film in the context of postmodernism.[2] There has even been talk of a remake of *Blackmail* by 20th Century-Fox, to be written by Charles Bennett, author of the play on which Hitchcock's film was based and contributor to the screenplay.

The trade press at the time of its release called *Blackmail* a 'film of outstanding merit',[3] a view echoed by reviewers with comments such as

'Best talking film yet – and British'.[4] The film was praised by critic Hugh Castle, editor of *Close Up* and a leading figure in the minority film culture, as 'perhaps the most intelligent mixture of sound and silence we have yet seen'.[5] But in 1929, the sound film was still a novelty, and most cinemas in Britain were yet to be equipped for sound. As with many films in this transitional period, both European and American, *Blackmail* was also released in a silent version, although not until the sound version had had a couple of months to impress audiences with its technical innovations. Understandably, the silent version has been overshadowed by the sound film, although as Charles Barr has noted, various critics – including Paul Rotha at the time and Eric Rohmer, Claude Chabrol and François Truffaut subsequently – make reference to it in their discussions of the original release version.[6]

As an early 'talkie', *Blackmail* is frequently described by film historians as a landmark film, an early attempt to incorporate new stylistic/technological dimensions into film-making.[7] The sound version belongs to a cluster of early sound films made between 1929 and 1931, including Lang's *M*, Sternberg's *Thunderbolt* and *The Blue Angel*, Pabst's *Kameradschaft* and Clair's *Sous les toits de Paris*, which marked out the various artistic options available through the addition of synchronised dialogue and sound. While the 'knife' sequence tends to dominate accounts of the film's novel use of sound, the historical significance of *Blackmail* lies more in the way in which it essays the possibilities of the new medium, and particularly in the way it contradicts the usual assumptions made by historians about the impact of sound on other aspects of film style. As Elisabeth Weis has noted:

> Whereas films of the period supposedly always showed the speaker because producers thought that the audience must see the source of sound, Hitchcock very often has the speaker off-screen. Whereas films were supposed to have been shot in long master shots [because sound could not be cut], Hitchcock only does so three times. Whereas cameras and people were supposed to remain immobile, Hitchcock moves his characters and his cameras during synchronised sequences.[8]

This alone makes the sound version of *Blackmail* a film of central importance to the history of cinema. But the silent version must be regarded as a significant contribution to silent film art.

Blackmail, then, is quintessential Hitchcock, a film which, according to *Cahiers du Cinéma* critics Rohmer and Chabrol, adumbrates many of the devices and themes of the director's subsequent more highly regarded American films. In historical terms, it *is* a landmark film in the development of cinema in the early sound period. Yet it is not simply frozen in the classic lineage of important films. In the 1980s, feminist critics such as Deborah Linderman and Tania Modleski have explored the picture from the point of view of psychoanalysis and sexual politics, while William Rothman drew attention to its modernist dimensions.[9] Like all great films, *Blackmail* resonates with meaning that is thrown into relief by changing historical and critical perspectives.

THE SOUND REVOLUTION?

How did *Blackmail* emerge? In what context was the film made? It was a context in which firmly established cinematic norms were being overturned by the advent of the new technology of sound. The transition from silent to sound cinema was relatively quick, especially when compared with, say, the shift from black and white to colour film. Yet it did take some time for the American film industry, and subsequently European cinema, to abandon completely the highly developed narrative and stylistic techniques of the silent film. Apart from the various experiments which had been conducted since the start of cinema in the mid-1890s, the earliest American sound pictures were Lee De Forest's Phonofilm programmes of 1923 and the Vitaphone shorts made by Warner Bros in 1926. In the same year Warners also released *Don Juan*, a feature film with specially composed music and sound effects synchronised with the film and supplied to exhibitors on discs. The film, together with its 'sound track', simply provided the kind of experience to which silent film audiences were accustomed: images accompanied by music and sound effects. The key difference, however, was that the sound accompaniment had been planned and controlled as integral to the film, and it was to be delivered from the projection box rather than from the orchestra pit or the Wurlitzer organ.

Films of the first wave of sound cinema such as *Don Juan*, and *Sunrise* (1927) and *Seventh Heaven* (1927) from the Fox Corporation, were basically silent films with musical scores and sound effects.[10] The same could be said of *The Jazz Singer*, released late in 1927, although crucially it did have two synchronised speech sequences, including Al Jolson's emblematic line, 'You ain't heard nothing yet.' It was these few seconds that marked it out from other sound films of the time. *The Jazz Singer* was a great success, but the major companies hesitated in the face of the several competing sound systems and the vast capital outlay necessary for the conversion to sound. However, in May 1928 the companies finally decided to shift definitively from silent to sound film and signed contracts with Western Electric for their Movietone system. Meanwhile Warners released the first all-dialogue American picture, *Lights of New York*. The shift was dramatic, and in 1929 Hollywood made more than 300 sound films.[11] By 1930, silent picture-making had virtually ceased in America, although many of the early talkies were also released in silent versions to cater for those cinemas yet to be wired for sound.[12]

In Britain, the first sound films were short pieces. According to Edmund Quarry, the 'first British talkie – a short, experimental domestic comedy – was screened during the winter of 1924–25, three years before the Americans came along with *The Jazz Singer*.'[13] Unfortunately Quarry, writing many years after the event, fails to name the film, although he does mention that it was made at a studio in Clapham and was 'shown at the British Empire Exhibition at Wembley and at one or two cinemas in the West End.' Better documented short sound films came a year or two later. In Britain, the De Forest Phonofilm process had been acquired in 1923, and the De Forest Phonofilms company began releasing short sound films, produced at a small studio in Clapham, at the end of 1926. The company continued to produce short subjects, including comedies, music hall acts and dramas, during 1927. Other sound companies were formed (like British Acoustic in 1926 and British Phototone in 1928), and during 1927 large exhibition chains such as PCT had organised demonstrations of the different sound systems.[14]

It was not until 1929, however, that the first British sound feature films emerged. There appear to be no equivalents of *Don Juan* and

Sunrise (feature films with integral music and sound effects) prior to 1929, although British Phototone did have plans to provide music and sound effects for British Instructional's *Underground*, directed by Anthony Asquith.[15] *The Jazz Singer* was not screened in Britain until September 1928, nearly a year after its American release, and it was not until the middle of 1929 that British sound films began to appear in any quantity. During that year British producers released a number of silent productions which had been hastily converted into sound pictures with the addition of dialogue scenes, music and sound effects, together with a smaller number of pictures conceived for sound. However, many films from that year remained silent, which was hardly surprising since few cinemas in Britain were converted to project sound films until the early 1930s. Only 22 per cent of cinemas had been converted by the end of 1929, and 37 per cent still remained unwired for sound at the end of 1930.[16]

The gradual introduction of sound in both the United States and Britain is a complicated matter, embracing problems of technology, rival patent clashes, different delivery systems (disc, various sound-on-film techniques) and their interchangeability, and the vast capital sums required to convert studios and theatres to the new medium. The wholesale change to sound pictures required substantial financial underwriting, and in America involved a battle between the giant communications companies Western Electric (a subsidiary of American Telephone and Telegraph) and the Radio Corporation of America (linked to General Electric). Most of the major companies took time to deliberate on the change to sound before signing contracts with Western Electric in 1928.

The delay was not just due to the complexities of business and finance. There was also the matter of aesthetic ideologies and debates about the impact of sound upon the kind of cinema that had evolved since 1895. Sound was seen by many as a threat to the subtle forms of art and communication developed in the absence of integral sound by the great film-makers of the 1910s and 1920s, including Hitchcock himself. The distinguished German director Friedrich Murnau had suggested that film 'ought ... to tell a complete story by means of images alone'.[17] Many years later, Hitchcock put this another way: film-makers, he said, 'should resort to dialogue only when it's impossible to do otherwise'.[18] Such maxims also reflected the thinking of the many film critics and theoreticians who resisted the advent of sound pictures, especially the dialogue film. Some influential film producers shared this view. In July 1928, Joseph M. Schenck, the chairman of United Artists, reportedly claimed that:

> Sound film will leave nothing to the intelligence of the picture going public. In the silent drama a certain gesture, a particular facial expression, will often convey more than a subtitle. But in talking films nothing will be left to the imagination, and for that reason they must only be a passing phase.[19]

From the mid-1920s onwards the British trade press carried many articles on the sound picture which debated its pros and cons and attempted to assess its future prospects. Opinion was mixed. Some

14   Hitchcock with Anny Ondra on the set

commentators forecast the shift to all-sound production that was to come; others dismissed the sound film as a novelty, or as a form best suited to short subjects and destined to remain ancillary to the silent film. Sidney Bernstein, founder of the Granada cinema chain, conducted the first of his famous questionnaires early in 1929, and the results revealed a great deal of public scepticism about the future of the sound film.[20] Producer Michael Balcon reflected in his autobiography about 'how thoroughly we deceived ourselves into believing that sound in relation to films was but a passing phase'; like other prominent producers of the time he had anticipated a continuing demand for silent films.[21] By 1929, however, Balcon was busy on a sound version of the successful play *Journey's End*, though he had to go to America to make the picture in the absence of sound facilities in his own studios.

Some saw the future in terms of a peaceful co-existence between the two types of film. In May 1928 *Kine Weekly*, whilst recognising that 'the sound film has achieved a widespread vogue in America', predicted separate development in Britain, with 'our kinemas divided into halls specialising some in the silent screen, others in the "talkies".'[22] And following a visit to the USA in 1929, John Maxwell (producer of *Blackmail*), reported:

> A question about the future of the silent picture brought the opinion that there would always be a market for them. Probably there will arise a general principle of showing one sound and one silent picture wherever there is a two picture programme. In this way one will act as a foil to the other, for, as a matter of fact, people would probably find two sound pictures at a sitting rather overpowering.[23]

Others were more prescient. J. C. Graham, an American who ran Famous Players-Lasky's distribution outlet in Britain, predicted a decline in the supply of silent pictures. Graham saw the sound film as an inevitable development, and suggested late in 1928 that film-makers who were 'short-sighted enough to try and set up in opposition to this mighty steam-roller will be crushed out of recognition and disappear from the entertainment world.'[24] In May 1929, Graham reiterated his support for sound films in an article with the unequivocal headline of

'Silent Film Dead'.[25] In the same month, however, *The Bioscope* carried an editorial warning that

> No greater mistake could be made than to suppose the silent film dead, or even to regard it as merely a 'second best' alternative to sound. It must be years before the new form of entertainment can supersede the older form.[26]

However, just a week later the editorial was changing its tune in a commentary on American producer Jesse Lasky's prophecy of the death of the silent film: 'He must be listened to.'[27] In July 1929, *The Bioscope* reported that the Cinematograph Exhibitors' Association, at their annual conference, had unanimously agreed that

> the Talking Film must be regarded not as a passing novelty, but as a permanent feature of the cinema entertainment, upon which it will certainly exercise a revolutionary influence and which it may ultimately dominate.[28]

In fact, 'talkies' – feature-length narratives with dialogue – had started to play in the few British cinemas wired for sound towards the end of 1928. *Kine Weekly* announced *The Terror* in November, citing it as the first 'talkie' presumably on the grounds that *The Jazz Singer* did not qualify as a fully fledged dialogue picture. At that time it was estimated that around forty cinemas in the country could show talking pictures. *The Singing Fool*, Jolson's follow-up to *The Jazz Singer*, was also released in November, *Kine Weekly* seeing it as 'the first worthwhile sound picture shown here';[29] and by the following spring the trade press was carrying advertisements which spelled out the box-office success of the film in various British cities.

The trade press soon began to note the increasing number of sound pictures. In April 1929, *Kine Weekly* commented that 'Talkies play a much bigger part than usual in this week's Trade Shows, which goes to prove which way the wind is blowing in America, even if it is only a breeze here at present.'[30] By May, with the breeze beginning to blow stronger, the journal had adopted a classification system to indicate which of the films reviewed were 'full talking', 'part talking' or 'silent'.

By July 1929, when the exhibitors met and deliberated on the new phenomenon, a number of American sound films had been released and were making an impact on British audiences. In addition, great American stars like Douglas Fairbanks, Mary Pickford and Ronald Colman had by this time made their 'talkie' debuts. And the 'first British all-talkie film', *Blackmail*, had been released.

In fact, in the midst of the early scepticism, there were a number of British film-makers whose interest in the sound picture dated back to 1928. However, one of the problems that the British film industry faced was the supply of sound equipment both for production and exhibition. In June 1928, the British Phototone Company was set up 'to exploit a system using twelve-inch discs and comparatively cheap reproduction equipment',[31] and in the same month it was reported that they had forty cinemas equipped and screening their sound pictures.[32] This was a start, but there were around 4,000 cinemas in Britain in the late 1920s. In July 1928, the trade press reported that 'many enquiries for Movietone installations are being made by exhibitors, but ... difficulties of delivery will not permit of installation being made in Great Britain for from two to three months.'[33]

On the production front, whilst leading producers like Michael Balcon were wary of British and European equipment and were prepared to wait until American equipment could be obtained, British Phototone had established links with a number of small production concerns. These included the Blattner Film Corporation, which in August 1928 announced plans for a sound production of *Carmen* to be made at their Elstree studios using the British Phototone equipment.[34] Although nothing was to come of this, the system was used by British Lion for their film *The Clue of the New Pin*, released in March 1929 and advertised by its distributor – Producers Distributing – as the first British 'All-Talkie'.[35]

Other film-makers, unwilling to wait until American equipment came to them, went to the equipment. Herbert Wilcox went to America in September 1928 to study sound films, and his company, British and Dominions, signed a contract to make sound films under Western Electric patents, the first British company to form such agreements. He remained in Hollywood for some time and produced a film, *Black Waters*, subsequently described in *Kine Weekly* as yet another 'first all-

British talkie'[36] despite the fact that it was made in America with American personnel. Victor Saville also went to America early in 1929 to re-shoot the last three reels of his silent picture *Kitty*, with dialogue written by Benn Levy, later to work as a scriptwriter on *Blackmail*. Released as a silent picture in January 1929, *Kitty* was re-released as a part-talkie in December of the same year. By early 1929, large companies such as Gainsborough, part of the large Gaumont British combine, were announcing that their future lay in sound pictures and that silent picture production would be discontinued.[37]

BRITISH INTERNATIONAL PICTURES

Hitchcock had been contracted to British International Pictures since 1927. His boss John Maxwell had been cautious in his public pronouncements on the future of the sound picture, but he too joined the trail to America to investigate the new phenomenon. In August 1928, *Kine Weekly*'s American correspondent reported that 'negotiations are taking place between the directors of RCA Photophone Inc., and John Maxwell of British International ... for the British right of the Photophone process of sound film.'[38] Indeed, the company report for the financial year 1928/29 stated:

> Last autumn the directors redesigned the new studios at Elstree then in construction with a view to making them sound-proof studios for the production of talking pictures. In January the necessary plant for making talking pictures was installed and in March the recording of full-length talking pictures started for the first time in this country at the company's studios.[39]

Clearly, British International was preparing for the move to sound picture production by the middle of 1928, prompted by the success in America of films like *The Jazz Singer* and its successor *The Singing Fool*. By early 1929 there were press reports about the imminent completion of the company's sound studios.[40] The crucial question of which system to adopt had yet to be settled, however, despite Maxwell's negotiations with RCA in 1928. In a speech to Manchester exhibitors in January

1929, Maxwell, while endorsing sound pictures and mentioning that 'he was told by his subsidiary in America that they must have sound films', was nevertheless evasive about finalising equipment plans.[41] In March 1929, *Kine Weekly* carried a major piece on British International's studio refurbishing plans and an interview with John Thorpe, general manager of the studio. Like Maxwell, Thorpe indicated a commitment to the sound film, though not without some hesitation. As the *Kine* correspondent wrote:

> Mr Thorpe ... discussed the sound film plans of British International with considerable caution and reserve. All 'talkie' activities are still in a distinctly vague and unsettled state and he obviously did not want to commit himself until plans could be more crystalised more definitely. This would probably not be until June, when it is hoped actual production can start in the main sound studios.[42]

This 'caution' may well be explicable in terms of problems of equipment supply or uncertainty over the competing systems, but it needs to be set against the fact that, despite the problems, the company did establish a temporary sound studio so that sound and talking sequences could be added to films currently in production. Indeed, a report in *The Bioscope* a week later included the comments that 'British International are not prepared to delay their entry into the realm of sound film production until June or July' and that 'exhaustive tests have encouraged BIP executives to schedule for immediate commencement a number of important dialogue features.'[43] The article went on to state that a 'start is being made with "Blackmail", Hitchcock's current production.... This is to have dialogue [sequences] written by Benn Levy and "Hitch" is commencing these this week.'[44]

The temporary studio – which was constructed inside another building – was small, with one stage about 40 by 70 feet with a 20-foot ceiling. The walls were hung with heavy flannelette material and the ceiling and floor treated with sound-absorbing materials. Although the studio was not entirely sound-proof, the company installed American sound equipment – RCA's Photophone system – and there were adjacent rooms for monitoring and recording sound. In addition,

28. PUB.7.

Shooting *Blackmail* at British International; a youthful Ronald Neame is behind the camera

another temporary studio was planned and Maxwell had hired two sound experts from the BBC, R. E. Jeffrey and D. F. Scanlan, who brought with them considerable experience of studio construction.[45]

Although there was undoubtedly a degree of caution in BIP's management, it is clear that managerial strategy had involved a shift to sound production, at least for part of the company's production schedules, from the middle of 1928; and the decision in early 1929 to go ahead with temporary sound studios indicates a desire to be ahead of the field. During this period the studios were visited by the Duke and Duchess of York, and the sound developments provided the centrepiece of their visit as they watched Hitchcock rehearse a dialogue sequence for *Blackmail*.[46]

THE PRODUCTION OF 'BLACKMAIL'

Blackmail was based on a play written by Charles Bennett first performed at the Globe Theatre in London early in 1928. The transfer of plays from the West End stage to film was an established practice in the British cinema of the time. Hitchcock himself had previously directed adaptations of Ivor Novello and Noël Coward for Gainsborough, and after *Blackmail* he filmed plays by O'Casey and Galsworthy.[47] Bennett himself worked with Hitchcock and Benn Levy on the script adaptation and, according to his own testimony, they were assisted by a young stills photographer at the studio. In his autobiography, Michael Powell claims to have worked on the script, although his name does not appear on the film's credits. Powell omits any mention of Bennett's scriptwriting contribution and also takes the credit for suggesting that the finale be set in the British Museum. In fact, he claims credit for creating the strategy associated with Hitchcock, of climaxing a film with a chase in a familiar and dramatic public setting.[48]

The cast was headed by Anny Ondra, a Polish-born actress who made her name in the Czechoslovakian silent cinema as a comic star, came to Britain in the late 1920s and appeared in two films directed by Graham Cutts as well as in Hitchcock's last silent film, *The Manxman*. However, the decision to make *Blackmail* in a sound version posed considerable production problems, since Anny Ondra's strong accent made her vocally unsuitable for the role of the lower middle-class shopkeeper's daughter.[49] Post-production dubbing was not available to Hitchcock and the solution was to have a British actress, Joan Barry, speak the lines from just off-camera whilst Ondra mimed to the camera. Joan Barry's refined Kensington tones may not perhaps accurately reflect the heroine's class, but the experiment just about paid off, with some critics seeing Ondra's slight hesitations in performance (doubtless due to problems of timing and synchronisation), as a positive contribution to the construction of Alice as a vulnerable victim.

The male lead, Ondra's detective boyfriend, was played by John Longden, a somewhat stolid leading man whose performance was in marked contrast to Anny Ondra's vivacity. The villain – the blackmailer Tracy – was played with considerable force by character actor Donald Calthrop, who specialised in playing unsavoury characters. Cyril Ritchard, a dancer and comedian, played the ill-fated artist, and the supporting cast included Irish actress Sara Allgood and Charles Paton as Alice's parents. A final member of the cast worth noting was ex-Detective Sergeant Bishop, 'late C.I.D. Scotland Yard', according to the credits, and no doubt chosen to guarantee authenticity as well as to play the detective in charge of the murder investigation.

Hitchcock was assigned to the project by John Maxwell, and *Blackmail* featured in British International's annual schedule announced in the trade press in January 1929.[50] The company's erection of temporary sound studios early in 1929 suggests a forward-looking studio organising itself for the changeover from silent to sound pictures. But subsequent accounts of the production of *Blackmail*, including the many sometimes contradictory versions offered by Hitchcock himself, cast the studio as conservative in its attitude towards the film. By contrast, Hitchcock presents himself as the wily artist subverting the front office. It is a familiar image, drawing on the powerful cinematic myth of the creative film author versus the philistine, money-conscious producer. In fact, a number of senior figures in the British cinema of the time, including Maxwell, had come into the industry from the hard-nosed world of film distribution, and they were not always sympathetic to the creative aspirations of the film-makers. Hitchcock himself had experienced problems with the distributor C. M. Woolf over the releasing of *The Lodger* a few years earlier. Woolf wanted to shelve the film, considering it too 'arty' for the general public, and this clash was undoubtedly to colour Hitchcock's attitude towards the production chiefs with whom he dealt.

Whatever the basis of the story, it has been fuelled by numerous subsequent accounts of the film's production. Scriptwriter Rodney Acland recalled that Hitchcock attributed *Blackmail*'s success to 'a scheme he had evolved for tricking the executive producers':

> The big shots couldn't stand the script of 'Blackmail' as Hitch wanted to shoot it: the characters were too real, the treatment too original. It had to be re-written in accordance with accepted film conventions. Determined not to be thwarted, Hitch, when he started work on the floor, went right ahead, so he told me, and shot the most important scenes as originally written. Outside the entrance to the sound-stage he had someone keeping close 'cave': at the approach of an executive producer, descending from his office to make sure that everything being shot was uninspired and conventional, this look-out man would dash in and give the director warning. Hitch would then be discovered directing the scene as re-written according to instructions.[51]

In this version of the film's production history, the studio bosses, although generally conservative in their attitude towards sound, decided during the shooting that the picture should have dialogue in the final reel. Presumably it would then have been released with a music and effects track and would turn into a talking picture near the end. This was a common strategy during the first half of 1929. A number of producers, sensing the impending changeover to talkies, hastily refurbished their completed or part-completed silent films by adding dialogue (usually to the final stages of the picture) so that they could be marketed as sound films. Hitchcock retrospectively claimed greater foresight, indicating in interviews that he arranged the shooting to provide him with material for an all-sound picture which he would be able to supplement with some reshooting. In his interviews with Truffaut, he says:

> I suspected the producers might change their minds and

eventually want an all-sound picture, I worked it out that way. We utilised the techniques of talkies, but without sound. Then, when the picture was complete, I raised objections to the part-sound version, and they gave me carte blanche to shoot some of the scenes over.[52]

Hitchcock's production strategy has been substantiated in Charles Barr's detailed comparison of the silent and sound versions of the picture, which reveals that while shooting the silent version of the film sanctioned by Maxwell, Hitchcock was also shooting separate takes of each shot in order to prepare a negative for the sound version of the film.[53] With British International's subsequent change of mind, he was quickly able to provide a sound version by using a mixture of the additional original silent footage post-dubbed with music and sound effects and newly shot dialogue sequences.[53] It was this version that was released some two months ahead of the silent version.

Hitchcock presents a similar tale of subterfuge and ingenuity in relation to the special effects cinematography used in the final part of the film, which is set in the British Museum. Lighting problems ruled out shooting in the museum itself and Hitchcock had to use the Schüfftan cinematographic process. The process was complicated, involving the use of mirrors and photographic transparencies or miniaturised sets which were combined in the filming with live action. That this could give a credible impression of action shot on location is demonstrated by the completed film. Yet according to Hitchcock, the process was treated with great suspicion by the BIP management and, in order to get the dramatic setting of the museum for the film's finale, Hitchcock had to resort to subterfuge. As John Russell Taylor has written, in a variation of the account given by Rodney Acland:

All this had to be done in great secrecy, because Maxwell was worried about how long the film was taking to shoot and no one in the studio management knew much about the Schüfftan process except that they mistrusted it as a new-fangled contraption which might well go wrong. As a cover, Hitch set up a second camera on the sidelines apparently photographing a letter. A lookout was posted, and if anybody from the front office was sighted approaching they would all drop what they were doing and suddenly be very intent on the letter until the danger was past.[54]

Yet the Schüfftan process had been in use at British International Pictures and its predecessor British National since the mid-1920s. British National had acquired the British rights to the technique and it was first used on the production of *Madame Pompadour*, directed by Herbert Wilcox in 1927.

The sophisticated development of such techniques had, in Rachael Low's words, 'revolutionised and greatly extended film production'.[55] It was no longer necessary to construct elaborate sets or to shoot on location when credible images such as those in the final sequences of *Blackmail* were obtainable through the use of one or other of the process methods. The introduction in 1929 of heavy sound cameras in their soundproof booths gave further impetus to the adoption of process cinematography, since it encouraged or even obliged film-makers to work entirely within the confines of the studio. The art directors on *Blackmail* were Wilfred Arnold and Norman Arnold, both of whom had considerable experience of process work. Indeed, Wilfred Arnold had already worked with the director on *The Ring* (Hitchcock's first picture for BIP), and the Schüfftan process had been used on that film. Such techniques were part of the established practice of the British film industry in the late 1920s, part of the technological context in which Hitchcock worked, and accounts of his allegedly secretive filming strategies need to be read in that context.

'BLACKMAIL': A CRITICAL HISTORY

By the middle of 1929, when *Blackmail* was released, Hitchcock had established a considerable reputation. After the release of *The Lodger* in 1926, he was regarded as the foremost young British film-maker and was fêted accordingly in the trade press and in the newspapers, which began to carry regular film columns during the 1920s. *The Ring* (1927) was hailed as 'the greatest production ever made in this country',[56] and much was expected of the director by the time *Blackmail* went into production in 1929. The press was not disappointed. *Kine Weekly* described the film as 'a splendid example of popular all-talkie screen entertainment', whilst *The Bioscope* proclaimed it as a 'film of outstanding merit'. Both reviews single out Hitchcock's direction, the writers displaying some sensitivity to the problems of directing talking pictures at this early point in their development. *The Bioscope* reviewer wrote that *Blackmail* was

> neither the mere adaptation of a stage play to the screen nor a silent film fitted with stage dialogue, and it may well be that Mr Hitchcock has solved the problem of combining the two and helped towards assigning the true position of the sound film in the ranks of entertainment.[57]

The American reception was variable, although *Variety* was clearly very interested in the film and provided two reviews. The first was filed from London on 1 July 1929 soon after the film's British release, the second some three months later after its presentation in New York. The London reviewer commended the film as

> not just a talker, but a motion picture that talks. Alfred J. Hitchcock has solved the problem of making a picture which does not lose any film technique and gains effect from dialog. Silent, it would be an unusually good film; as it is, it comes near to being a landmark.[58]

Blackmail was seen as a potential influence on the course of the talking picture, the writer predicting that the film would 'have much the same effect on American techniques that some of the German films had half a dozen years ago.' In an echo of many comments on the film, the story is dismissed as 'impossible', but the production and acting are praised. The 'knife' sequence is singled out as 'a good effect', but the reviewer has a dig at Hitchcock's status as film artist and draws attention to the elaborate staircase set: 'Hitchcock still cannot get away from the staircase complex he found in "The Lodger". So many of the sobbers raved about his "art" he believes it consists in long, winding staircases!' The reviewer concludes that *Blackmail* 'at this stage of talkers, mighty near the best yet. But with the certainty of quick developments in talking technique, it needs a quick release.'

Unfortunately, quick American release was denied, and the second *Variety* review three months later, although praising the film as 'a creditable British output', found that it did not compare with the fast-developing American sound film. Lined up against *Blackmail* was 'the race of the American talker, its easy supremacy and just at this moment a remarkable line-up of domestic pictures that ordinarily might keep any foreign-made of an average such as here out of the first runs, until the native supply has been exhausted.'[59] The key to success in the American market was a Broadway opening at one of the showcase cinemas of the major Hollywood companies, and this the film failed to secure. *Kine Weekly* outlined the problems:

'Blackmail' is a good picture, comparable to America's best, but it contains no star of international, or American reputation, nor has it been well-publicised. During its run at the Capitol the press campaign was inadequate and did little to help it on its way. It has only the fine press notices that helped it achieve its success. The poster display suggested a serial rather than a British talkie masterpiece, while the individual artistes never received the publicity their respective performances merited.[60]

Blackmail did enjoy some success in the United States, establishing a house record in the Davis Theatre in San Francisco.

What success *Blackmail* achieved in America was indeed helped by the press notices. Hitchcock's relationships with the press were carefully cultivated, and his biographers refer to his stance taken early in his career that films should be made not for the public or the distributors or the exhibitors but for the press.[61] Following the success of *Blackmail*, Hitchcock set up a company to handle his publicity, Hitchcock Baker Productions, formed for 'the sole task of advertising to the press the newsworthiness of Alfred Hitchcock, producer-director'.[62]

Less controllable, however, and perhaps more dependent upon the actual films, were his relationships with the more specialised film critics and writers. The 1920s had seen the development in Britain of what later became known as a 'minority film culture', a loose though retrospectively discernible configuration of institutions and individuals bound together by a taste for European 'art' films and, in the 1930s, documentary pictures. This cultural grouping included the London-based Film Society, set up in 1925, and the nationwide film society movement which followed. The Film Society also encouraged the growth of commercially run 'art' cinemas, both in London and other cities, which formed a network of alternative screening venues during the 1920s and 1930s. Art cinema audiences also had their own journals, *Close Up* and its successors *Cinema Quarterly* and *World Film News*. Along with the interest in art cinema and documentary film went a dismissal of most of the popular cinema of Hollywood and a deep critical suspicion of British cinema. These views were reflected in the programming policies of the Film Society, the editorial tone of *Close Up*, and the aesthetic orientation of books such as Paul Rotha's *The Film Till Now* (1930).

What did *Blackmail* mean to a film culture which in its critical stance had implicitly established a high art film/popular film divide? It was at best grudging respect. The highbrow critics wriggled: they recognised the film's cinematic qualities, its affinities with the respected European 'art' cinemas, and its sophisticated form, but it was still a product of the critically disreputable British commercial cinema – and a genre film to boot. *Close Up*'s Hugh Castle began his review by suggesting that '*Blackmail* is perhaps the most intelligent mixture of sound and silence we have yet seen,' then delivered his judgment that the film 'is not a great picture, it is not a masterpiece, it is not an artistic triumph, it is not a valuable addition to the gallery of the world's great films, it is not even, I think, a great box-office picture.' Although calling the film 'a first effort of which the British industry has every reason to be proud', his review ended with condescension:

> Within twenty-four hours of the show being over, the optimists were predicting an immediate revival in British production. *Blackmail* has put us on top of the world. Pudovkin is dead, Eisenstein has ceased to be. Even Carl Laemmle, a greater figure than either, is forgotten for the moment!
> We shall see.[63]

Close Up returned to the film in October 1929, in a long and closely argued editorial by Kenneth Macpherson which took as its starting point the notion that 'those who have mentioned *Blackmail* in *Close Up* have left much to say about it.'[64] In particular, Macpherson echoed Castle's view that *Blackmail* included passages of film-making which integrated image and sound more successfully than its talkie contemporaries and which signalled 'the first sign of a comprehension of the relationship of techniques'. Macpherson was specifically impressed by the cut from the shot of Alice recoiling at the sight of the sleeping beggar's outstretched hand to the shot of Crewe's landlady screaming. 'This is neat and dramatic. It is important, because it is the exact use of sound in its right relation.' Interestingly, in the context of a film culture which usually considered the techniques of silent film superior, Macpherson thought the handling of the sequence benefited from the use of sound:

> The scream that was both the girl's scream and the concierge's scream banished a lot that we can well do without. Picture this silent. You could not very well leave Anny Ondra screaming there. The beggar would or would not wake. She would hurry on. This would probably have to be shown. At the point of her hurrying on there could be a cut to the bed curtain being pulled back and then the old woman's face screaming. That is to say, that at least there would have had to be three additional un-

Cutting from Alice's recoil at the sight of the beggar to the landlady's discovery of the body

dramatic shots needful to continuity, but causing a sagging of dramatic moment.

Most attacks on the early talkies were couched in terms of the superiority of the silent film, but here is an argument in favour of the potential communicative and dramatic economy of the pertinent use of sound. In fact, in the silent version Hitchcock did use the same or very similar shots in the same sequence; the difference between the two versions is the overlapping scream. A few months later, however, *Close Up* was again publishing more grudging opinions. The American critic Harry Alan Potamkin regarded the film as the 'best planned talkie I have yet seen', but went on: 'The English are inflating the importance of the film. It has no real meaning and is poor suspense filming.... Its competence is only competence after all, for Hitchcock is not a singularly inventive mentality.'[65] Potamkin, like many writers who lived through the transition from silent to sound cinema, was sceptical about the new technique and thought that the dialogue film would ultimately disappear – views he was still expressing in 1930.

Paul Rotha's *The Film Till Now* was both a history of cinema from its origins to the early sound period and a manifesto for the silent film. The book embodies the visual aesthetic ideology of the silent period. After proclaiming that 'the most dramatic possible method of telling a story is by a succession of pictures,' Rotha went on to reflect upon the advent of the sound picture:

> The attempted combination of speech and picture is the direct opposition of two separate mediums, which appeal in two utterly different ways. If the two are wedded, one must be subordinated to the other, and at once division of appeal will occur. For this reason a silent visual film is capable of achieving a more dramatic, lasting, and powerful effect on an audience by its singleness of appeal than a dialogue film, in which the visual image is, at its best, a photograph of the voice. *Blackmail*, one of the so-called good dialogue films, will be completely forgotten in a few months by those who have seen it.[66]

Rotha was not completely dismissive of *Blackmail*, even if his grudging tone echoed that of Castle and Macpherson in *Close Up*. Like Potamkin, he thought the film lacked meaning. It was 'handicapped by poor narrative interest', yet despite 'the inevitable restrictions of dialogue, nevertheless showed Hitchcock in a progressive mood. His much commented upon use of sound as an emphasis to the drama of the visual image was well conceived, but inclined to be over-obvious.' Rotha's comments were made after viewings of both the sound and silent versions, and he concludes that 'the silent version was infinitely better than the dialogue, the action being allowed its proper freedom.'[67]

Such views were in keeping with the general opinion of Hitchcock as a director in the early 1930s – perhaps best summed up by John Grierson's comment that 'Hitchcock is no more than the world's best director of unimportant pictures.'[68] The problem most highbrow critics had with Hitchcock was that while they recognised his techniques and his artistic strategies ('master of detail', 'the Hitchcock touch'), they invariably expressed disappointment with the themes and subject matter of his films. *Blackmail* was no exception: a mere thriller, a genre piece, redeemed somewhat by incidental detail such as the 'knife' sequence but basically devoid of serious meaning. Grierson, understandably from his documentary perspective, wanted Hitchcock to harness his grasp of cinema to specifically social ends. He hoped that the director would soon relinquish the escapist world of popular genres and West End stage adaptations and 'give us a film of the potteries or of Manchester or of Middlesbrough – with the personals in their proper places and the life of a community instead of a benighted lady at stake.'[69] *Blackmail*, of course, is a 'benighted lady' film *par excellence*.

The Film Society acknowledged the importance of *Blackmail* as a contribution to early sound picture-making by including a short extract from the film as part of its early 1932 compilation programme, 'Examples of Sound Film Technique', illustrating 'early experiments in the dramatic emphasis of sound'.[70] Hitchcock's work had been screened previously by the society, although also in extract form. In a 1931 performance, the opening scenes of *The Lodger* were contrasted with the auction scene from *The Skin Game* – Hitchcock's fourth sound picture – in order to compare silent and sound film techniques.[71] *Blackmail* was revived in 1936 in a series of programmes on the history of cinema at the Everyman Cinema in London, where it was shown with Lewis

Milestone's *The Front Page* as an example of an early talkie. It was also the subject of a brief piece in 1937 by film-maker Harry Watt in the documentarists' paper *World Film News*.[72] Watt praised the film for a 'freshness about the approach to sound ... that is positively startling in these days of stereotyped dialogue and balanced background.' Like most writers on the film, he draws attention to the sound highspots – the cut from Anny Ondra's face to the shrieking face of the landlady, the 'knife' sequence, the piercing clang of the shop doorbell which heralds the arrival of the blackmailer. Interestingly, for a documentary realist, Watt defends the expressionist distortions of the soundtrack:

> All through the film there occur these imaginative uses of sound. They may be criticised as unreal but in point of fact they are not. Every one helped to get across to the audience the reality of the girl's terror, the reality of her suspense. Why should sound on the screen always be real? We all know that a door bangs or a clock ticks. But what we should want to hear is how the noises sound to the characters we are seeing.

Watt was one of the 1930s documentarists who leaned towards fictional narrative and the story-documentary aimed at the large cinema audience. Eventually he moved to feature film-making, including a stint with Hitchcock on *Jamaica Inn* (1939).

The film culture that emerged from the 1920s and 1930s was heavily influenced both by notions of film art as represented by the classics of the European silent film and by the social commitments of the documentary movement of the 30s. *Blackmail* shared the experimentalism of the former, and can be linked to the documentary impulse through, for example, the sequences early in the film which sketch the criminal's environment. The 1940s brought influential books on cinema by Roger Manvell and Ernest Lindgren, and publications such as *The Penguin Film Review*. *Blackmail* earns a few mentions in these publications.

The first issue of *The Penguin Film Review* included a piece by Anthony Asquith surveying the development of film narrative. Hitchcock's early sound films are cited as important instances of creative early talkies, and *Blackmail*'s 'knife' sequence is singled out as an appropriate way of subjectivising the experience of the spectator. Asquith writes, 'Just as in silent films we saw that we could identify the eye of the audience with that of one of the characters in the film, so in sound films we can identify the ear, and not only the physical ear but the emotional ear, with the ear of the audience.'[73] Ernest Lindgren's *The Art of the Film*, first published in 1948, also analysed the 'knife' sequence but was somewhat disturbed by its expressionism or, to use Lindgren's term, its use of 'non-naturalistic sound'. Lindgren argued that 'where the film-maker can secure the result he wants by the relating of images and sounds singled out by selection from the natural circumstances of the scene, the result is likely to be more forceful and convincing than if he introduces sound effects adventitiously.'[74] Lindgren was much happier with the fluid cutting of images in the earlier parts of the film, and in particular he mentions the sequence at the beginning of the narrative in which the criminal is arrested. He describes the array of intercut images, and comments that the 'spectator of the film, considered as a spectator, is no longer stationary as in the theatre; he is made by the art of editing an active observer, moving about in the midst of the action wherever the director chooses to lead him.'[75] Lindgren reflects in this passage the great respect that British film culture had for a cinema based on editing and deriving from the silent films of Griffith and the Soviet film-makers.

Lindgren, along with Roger Manvell, whose influential *Film* (1944) surprisingly omits any mention of *Blackmail*, represent the critical orthodoxy of the period. A challenge to their attitudes came in 1946 with the establishment of the journal *Sequence*. In a study of Hitchcock in a 1949 issue, Lindsay Anderson comments on the celebrated sound sequences, but he also identifies a certain 'realism' in the *mise en scène*: 'The everyday locales – a Corner-House restaurant, the police station, the little tobacconist's shop where the heroine lives with her parents, empty London streets at dawn – are authentic.'[76] Anderson's comments echo Grierson's admiration for the realist touches in the films of the silent and early sound period, and he also pinpoints Hitchcock's skilful handling of 'incident and narrative'. Hitchcock is an entertainer and 'has never been a "serious" director.'

A new perspective on Hitchcock emerged in the 1950s in the French journal *Cahiers du Cinéma* and, in particular, from the critics Eric

Rohmer and Claude Chabrol whose study of Hitchcock's films was published in 1957. Their interpretations constituted a formidable challenge to their critical predecessors, who had failed to perceive any substantial content in the films. They also took issue with critics who regarded the British films as superior to the American films, although they conceded that 'though we consider these apprentice years to be somewhat less significant than other critics find them, a number of Hitchcock's early films are not unworthy of those that were to follow.'[77] The key difference, however, lay in their presentation of Hitchcock as a Catholic moralist, as a director whose films were an embodiment of quite profound ideas. British critics, by and large, had conceded that Hitchcock was ingenious in terms of technique and form but that he had little to say. The Rohmer/Chabrol position depended upon collapsing the traditional distinction between form and content, and their study concludes with the following bold, and influential, judgment:

> Hitchcock is one of the greatest *inventors of form* in the entire history of cinema. Perhaps only Murnau and Eisenstein can sustain comparison with him when it comes to form. Our effort will not have been in vain if we have been able to demonstrate how an entire moral universe has been elaborated on the basis of this form and by its very rigor. In Hitchcock's work form does not embellish content, it creates it. All of Hitchcock can be summed up in this formula.[78]

Their analysis of *Blackmail* refers to Hitchcock's 'overflowing imagination in his use of sound', but the focus is on theme and content. They mention 'the moral positions of the protagonists', the use of 'cinematic means to impose the point of view from which it was to be seen', Alice's '*moral* punishment', 'the description of a woman's torments, which was to be one of the important themes of the early Hollywood years', and 'the famous notion of the "transfer" of guilt'.[79] The analysis leaves discussion of the formal innovations of the soundtrack to the end, preferring to foreground the moral message of the film. Where most critics had seen the film as, at most, a demonstration of technical bravura, the Rohmer/Chabrol account was in line with the *Cahiers du Cinéma* approach, combining a strong interest in form and style with a sense of directorial vision and theme. It was this tradition of criticism that was to elevate Hitchcock to the world cinematic pantheon, and to frame the discussion of his work within Anglo-Saxon criticism in the 1960s.

The Hitchcock who emerged from *Cahiers du Cinéma*, and from British and American critics influenced by it, was based mainly upon his American films. Robin Wood's *Hitchcock's Films*, echoing Rohmer and Chabrol, considered the British films 'so overshadowed by his recent development as to seem, in retrospect, little more than 'prentice work, interesting chiefly because they are Hitchcock's.'[80] Wood's focus on the American films reflected the general interest in Hollywood cinema (and apparent lack of interest in British cinema history) within Anglo-American film culture during the 1960s. *Blackmail*, along with Hitchcock's twenty-two other British films, largely disappeared from critical interest.

The reinstatement of British Hitchcock and *Blackmail* as a focus of critical interest came in the context of structuralist criticism and, especially, the structuralist criticism that was influenced by psychoanalysis and concerned with questions of gender and sexuality. Criticism in the 1960s had established Hitchcock as a dramatist of the malevolence which lurks just beneath the surface of life. Peter Wollen, for example, wrote of the 'chaos-world' on to which many Hitchcock films opened. Wollen gave this admittedly commonplace thematic preoccupation a psychoanalytical dimension, suggesting that Hitchcock's cinema was constituted by 'the rhetoric of the unconscious, the world which surges up beneath the thin protection offered us by civilisation.'[81]

Films such as *Blackmail* fit snugly into this account of the Hitchcockian world, with its nondescript couple becoming embroiled in a horror world of death, blackmail and undischarged guilt. All this in the context of a lover's tiff about a trip to the pictures over tea in a Lyons Corner House! As Charles Barr has pointed out, the British films, 'though they lack the richness of *mise en scène*, and of character creation and acting, that were so important to Robin Wood and *Movie*, are rich precisely in those elements which make Hitchcock so important to a new and very productive school of structuralist and psychoanalytic criticism.'[82] Barr points up the complex relationship that Hitchcock's films – both British and American – have to the norms and conventions of the Hollywood classical style; and he draws attention to the ways in which some of the British pictures are marked by 'powerful Oedipal stories', 'play with point of view and fantasy' and possess an 'intensely "interior" quality'. Whereas earlier critics had looked at the exterior referential aspects of *Blackmail* – the well-observed backstreets, the Lyons Corner House, the tobacconist's shop, the realism of the *mise en scène* – recent critics have been more interested in the ways in which the film probes an interior world of fantasy and desire and yields a range of covert, repressed and symbolic meanings available to a film culture less restricted by the critical precepts of realism.

In her book *The Women Who Knew Too Much*, Tania Modleski's analysis of *Blackmail* is designed to demonstrate 'the extent to which the film undermines patriarchal law and creates sympathy for and identification with the female outlaw'.[83] Robin Wood's *Hitchcock's Films Revisited* supplements his original 1965 text with critical readings influenced by more recent film theory. Although Wood in his original book had passed hastily over the director's British career, the revised version contains a number of articles on the British films, including a substantial essay on *Blackmail* which highlights its complex relationship to the norms of classical film style and to patriarchal ideology. Barr's point about the suitability of the British films for such analysis is amply borne out by Wood's 'conversion'.

'BLACKMAIL': A CRITICAL ANALYSIS

Blackmail opens on a vertiginous image of a spinning hub cap which is to draw the audience into the familiar Hitchcockian nightmare world of sex and violence, killing and deception. The opening sequence, which runs for around ten minutes, delays the onset of the central fictional concern and oscillates between a sort of documentary on police procedures and an action picture of a police chase. Although *Blackmail* was heralded as Britain's first talkie, the opening eschews dialogue in favour of expository inserts of messages, door signs and so on. This is partly due to the film's hybrid origins as both a silent and a sound picture; other early British talkies also withheld the dialogue until well into the film to highlight the moment of its arrival.

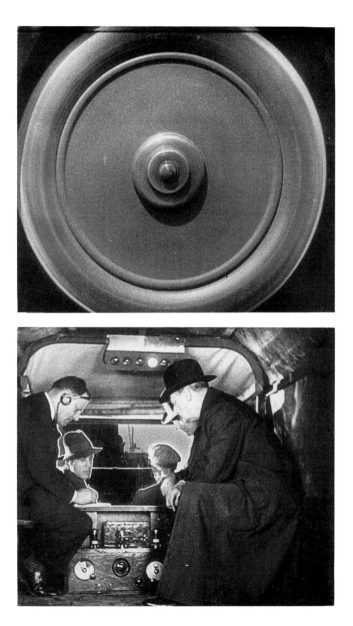

The opening sequence leading to the arrest

The opening sequence is a compendium of the art of the silent film. The spinning hub cap gives way to a number of shots of a speeding lorry, including a subjective travelling shot as the lorry hurtles through the streets of London. Interwoven shots from inside the lorry show the radio equipment being used by the police. The montage of images and the musical soundtrack convey an urgency which is underscored by a graphic insert showing the address of the suspect: in the manner of a silent film, the single insert shot makes clear what the images suggest. As we move further into the sequence, Hitchcock deploys various styles of presentation that derive from key silent film traditions. The lorry arrives at the suspect's home and as the police approach his room, the stylistic reference is the German silent cinema. In a series of close shots, the policemen's faces are crossed by narrow shadows, their threatening presence and the sense of tension conveyed by expressionist framing and lighting. As the scene develops, there is a complex interplay of point-of-view shots which owes more to the classical silent cinema technique of cross-cutting to create suspense. The sequence continues with the interrogation of the suspect at New Scotland Yard, the protracted timescale conveyed in pure silent cinema terms with a shot of an ashtray containing a single cigarette dissolving into a shot of the ashtray filled with several cigarette butts. The arrested man is locked in a cell, his imprisonment similarly rendered in a series of close-ups of significant detail together with some explanatory 'title' shots – a door bearing the word 'cells', a document which outlines the identification parade procedure, and so on. The events are constructed from a range of small details according to the rules of narrative construction in the silent cinema codified by such theorists as Pudovkin.

Hitchcock's résumé of silent narrative techniques can also be seen as a skilful documentary-style sequence. The careful exposition of the mechanics of detection, especially the detail of the wireless equipment which guides the police to their quarry, gives way to an equally detailed presentation of the procedures of arrest and imprisonment, with documentary-style attention given to finger-printing, 'mug' shots and the identification parade. The documentary aspect is also present in the arrest itself, with the seedy context of criminal life, the drab environment in which the suspect lives, presented with considerable 'realistic' detail. The police are shown arriving at an archway through which we see men hanging around talking, children playing and a horse and cart. The images are full of residual detail, elements which simply serve to provide a surface authenticity, a palpable feel of the real world. A subsequent image shows the children playing together and women talking as they hang out washing and clean windows.

Images such as these have little to do with the progress of the narrative and can be regarded as an attempt to create the social context from which the criminal emerges. In addition, there is a hint of sympathy with the criminal when a stone is hurled at the police through the window of his room. A social commentary is sandwiched between the cold, objective 'documentary' presentation of the chase and the interrogation and imprisonment. It was elements such as these which caught the attention of John Grierson and Lindsay Anderson. Grierson referred to Hitchcock as 'the only English director who can put the English poor on the screen with any verisimilitude',[84] while Anderson was impressed by the director's 'conscientious realism ... of locales and characters.'[85] As Raymond Durgnat was later to comment on these realist vignettes:

> ... it must be remembered that realism in the '30s was a rarer and more difficult achievement, that the director couldn't just point a TV camera in the street. He had first to notice certain details, love them enough to remember and recreate them, and lastly to slide them deftly into the thriller context.[86]

Documentary-style openings had become a feature of Hitchcock's early films. The openings of *The Lodger* (1926), *The Ring* (1927) and *The Manxman* (1928) are like brief documentaries about the dissemination of dramatic news, fairground life and the fishing industry respectively. The verisimilitude was not confined to the criminal environment. The police headquarters constructed in the BIP studios was 'a very carefully and authentically reconstructed replica of the anteroom and corridors of Scotland Yard as it is today', according to P. L. Mannock, Studio Correspondent of *Kine Weekly*. Mannock had escorted Major General Sir Wyndham Childs, ex-head of the CID, around the set of *Blackmail* and, as he reported, 'His observant eye detected hardly any discrepancy from the original and he identified his own room almost before we arrived by Jack Cox's camera. The attention to detail impressed him very favourably...'[87]

For all its documentary flavour, the opening sequence does include characters subsequently identified in the narrative. In particular, Frank Webber (John Longden), one of the arresting officers, has a key role as the boyfriend of the central character, Alice White (Anny Ondra), although he is not singled out here in any specific way. Hitchcock's original idea for the film revolved round the simple notion of a conflict between love and duty; as he wrote a few years after the film's release, the 'hazy pattern one saw beforehand was duty – love – love versus duty – and finally either duty or love.'[88] What he wanted to stress in the opening reel was the general theme of duty, with the policemen simply going about their business in a detached manner.

> I showed the arrest of a criminal by Scotland Yard detectives, and tried to make it as concrete and detailed as I could. You even saw the detectives take the man to the lavatory to wash his hands – nothing exciting, just the routine of duty.[89]

Having established 'duty', the film next establishes 'love', although in a tense and turbulent way, in the sequence where Frank meets Alice and takes her to a Lyons Corner House. In fact, Hitchcock's plan was to play with these themes and to end the film with Alice's arrest and a repeat of the opening, this time with Frank putting his girlfriend through the procedures of arrest, interrogation and imprisonment. Duty would be seen to triumph over love, giving the film a satisfying formal symmetry with the ending replying to the beginning in a manner which many critics see as typical of classical cinema. Hitchcock did not get his way entirely because the producers considered such an ending too downbeat for audiences. However, the film does return to New Scotland Yard at the end, with Alice's arrest for murder at least a possibility.

With the arrested man behind bars, Frank goes off duty and meets Alice, who is waiting for him at the police station entrance. Frank is late and Alice is edgy with him whilst sharing a private joke with the policeman on the door. She laughs with the policeman and frowns at Frank almost simultaneously, creating a slight tension between them which prepares the ground for their subsequent argument in the café. By this point dialogue has been introduced, but although Alice does petulantly complain to Frank for keeping her waiting the atmosphere between them owes more to Anny Ondra's repertoire of gestures than to what she actually says. As they leave the station to walk to the underground, a line of slowly marching policemen crosses between them and the camera – a slightly disturbing and distracting image at this point.

A single-shot set-up of an underground train ride moves the narrative on in conventional fashion as Frank and Alice start their evening out. Conventional, that is, apart from one key element: it is here that Hitchcock makes his own appearance in the film. It was not his first screen appearance, but it is one in which he does a little more than simply cross the screen or act as an extra in a crowd. As Maurice Yacowar has pointed out, Hitchcock is privileged in the *mise en scène* and photographed facing the camera with the principal characters in profile. He is trying to read a book, but a little boy pulls his hat over his ears whilst he remonstrates with the boy's mother. Such appearances were of course to become Hitchcock's artistic trademark, though they are usually restricted to walk-ons.

The next sequence takes place in a Lyons Corner House, and again Hitchcock sought authenticity by shooting some of the sequence on location in London's West End at the Lyons Corner House in Coventry Street. The scene, which is quite long, develops the acrimony between Frank and Alice and ends on her fateful departure with the artist Crewe (Cyril Ritchard). In marked contrast to the fluidity of the opening sequences, the dining room scene almost slows the film to a halt with lengthy takes of the conversation between Frank and Alice. It is here that we can see the impact of dialogue shooting on scenic construction in these early days of the talkies. The scene is made up of twenty shots and lasts just over four and a half minutes. The dominant impression is one of 'photographs of people talking',[90] and an analysis of the sequence confirms this. Almost three and a half minutes of screen time are taken up by four shots of Frank and Alice in a profile two-shot at the table. The remaining minute or so contains sixteen shots, all quite brief, including shots of the couple walking to the table, an insert of Alice's note from her artist friend, and the exchange of 'meaningful' close-ups when he arrives to keep their rendezvous.

The fluid cross-cutting of these close-ups contrasts with the somewhat static set-up which characterises most of the sequence. Early sound recording techniques meant that synchronised dialogue had to be recorded simultaneously with the image and – before the self-blimped camera became available to British film-makers – the camera had to be enclosed in a sound-proofed booth. There was also the problem of Anny Ondra's foreign accent, and Hitchcock's shooting had to accommodate the novel technique of the actress miming her dialogue whilst it was actually being spoken just off-camera by Joan Barry. These were considerable restrictions, and the sequence bears out the conventional wisdom about films of this period that dialogue sequences meant fixed-camera set-ups with little or no camera or actor movement. However, as Elisabeth Weis has demonstrated, *Blackmail* contains a number of dialogue sequences which are handled differently, incorporating the more dynamic techniques developed in the silent film.

However static, the sequence is pivotal to the narrative. The couple begin with a trivial discussion about Alice's torn glove which she has left on another table. They have arranged to go to the cinema and Frank wants to see the new Scotland Yard picture, *Fingerprints*. Their discussion of the film is amusingly reflexive as Alice claims that no one would have heard of Scotland Yard had it not been for Edgar Wallace. Frank muses that the film will probably have all the details wrong, but Alice comments that it should be authentic since a criminal has been hired to direct it. *Blackmail* itself may have guaranteed its 'realist' credentials in similar fashion by having an ex-CID officer in the cast playing, appropriately enough, a Detective Sergeant. At first, Alice does not want to go to the cinema, having arranged a meeting with another of her admirers, who turns out to be the artist Crewe. He fails to appear at the appointed time, so she agrees to accompany Frank, only to change her mind again when Crewe finally arrives. Driven to distraction, Frank stalks off. He calms down outside, but just as he turns back Alice goes off with Crewe, leaving Frank a stunned bystander. The narrative is up and running. A conflict – a love triangle – has been introduced, though at this point Frank disappears from the film.

We then move to later in the evening, as Crewe takes Alice home. First, however, we see an unidentified location, a large house, with a man, also as yet unidentified, standing to the left of the frame beneath a lamp-post. He moves out, back in, then out of frame again as Alice and Crewe enter from the opposite side. A cut to a closer shot of the couple allows us to hear their conversation. Crewe's studio apartment is close to Alice's home and he invites her to see it. Eventually he agrees, but during their conversation we cut to a close shot of the man lurking nearby. Before they go in, he calls to Crewe and they have a brief inaudible conversation off-screen. Crewe dismisses him as a sponger. It is a disconcerting episode which only makes sense in retrospect.

The couple climb to Crewe's attic studio by way of a cut-out, full-size staircase set with the camera rising with them. It is a bravura shot, which may relate to the German influence on Hitchcock and specifically to what Lotte Eisner called the 'obsession with staircases' in German silent cinema.[91] Hitchcock had directed his early features in Germany and *Blackmail*, along with *The Lodger*, betrays a debt to the dark,

The bravura shot of the staircase

obsessive world of the German silent film. Whatever its origins, however, like many a shot in Hitchcock's cinema it draws attention to itself and momentarily arrests the narrative flow. Once inside the artist's studio, we move towards the explosive event on which the film turns. Alice has previously expressed her trust in Crewe and her decision to go back to his studio is based on an innocent inquisitiveness. The broad cultural connotations of such an invitation are of course clear to the audience, but once in the studio Hitchcock sets about constructing Alice's descent into nightmare in quite specific ways.

After some small talk, she glances from the window into the street and sees a policeman walking by. Another glance, and then there is a close shot of a mocking jester figure. Although the camera soon pulls back to reveal it as a painting in the studio, its first appearance suggests one of those symbolic motifs used in the Soviet silent film to comment on narrative action. The jester arrives unheralded, but the

The close-up of the jester

shot interacts in quite specific ways with the previous images of Alice looking out of the window. It is part of an allusive chain of discourse about her predicament. The glance at the policeman evokes Frank, her abandoned policeman boyfriend, but her rather nervous reaction also suggests her uncertainty about the invitation to the studio. The image of the mocking jester confirms her presence as unwise. The painting theme continues as Alice starts to play with a palette and brush and makes a mark on a blank canvas. Crewe encourages her and she paints a face on the canvas. It is an unskilled rendition, like a child's painting, and Crewe helps her finish it by sketching a nude female body on to the head, a sketch which accurately embodies a distinction – childlike woman/sophisticated man – between the two characters. Indeed, Alice's subsequent behaviour includes changing into a ballet dress/child's party frock and skipping around the studio like a child playing. While she is changing, Crewe sings a Noël Coward-like song, 'Miss Up to Date',

Dividing the frame as an alternative to montage: Alice changes her dress

which includes the line, 'They say you're wild, a naughty child.' Crewe stresses that the song is about Alice.

The scene began with a montage construction involving the image of the policeman and the jester painting, but the style changes as montage is replaced by lengthy single takes with both characters together in frame. The change is partly owed to the increased importance of dialogue and song in the middle of the scene; but whereas the earlier dialogue scenes in the Lyons Corner House are shot quite functionally, the scene in which Alice changes into the frock indicates Hitchcock thinking through alternatives to montage. He divides the screen space, with Alice on the right behind a screen which bisects the film frame and Crewe left of frame at the piano singing to her. Shortly after this the narrative takes its sinister turn. Crewe kisses Alice but is rebuffed. Alice's childish demeanour alters dramatically and she prepares to change back into her dress. Crewe renews his assault,

Alice after the killing

dragging her towards the curtained-off bed. We see the curtains reverberate with the struggle, Alice's hand reaches out and grabs a breadknife on the bedside table, a further struggle, then Crewe's limp hand falls from the bed – an image used subsequently as an element in Alice's nightmare recollections of the event. Alice emerges in a state of shock and retrieves her dress. It is draped over the jester painting, and when she pulls it off she is once again confronted by the mocking gesture which warned her earlier. She sets off as in a dream – or nightmare. The staircase is now shown from high above, in one of those vertiginous shots that Hitchcock was to build into a number of his later films. Alice moves off into the night, but the camera lingers and across the door falls the shadow of a man. The sequence ends as it had begun, outside Crewe's apartment with the shadowy figure skulking but still unidentified.

Alice sets off, as we think, for home. In fact, although her home is close, she spends all night wandering through the streets, through West End theatreland, across Trafalgar Square and so on, as if in a trance. The nightmare is constructed through a variety of expressionist techniques, with Hitchcock both running through his repertory of silent film techniques and introducing sound effects in ways which were to attract considerable attention from a critical community basically suspicious of sound. As Alice crosses the road, the outstretched hand of the traffic policeman is intercut with the image of Crewe's hand. She then glances at some neon signs and an animated cocktail shaker becomes the knife plunging into Crewe's body. Night passes and Alice is still wandering. As she walks along, the dead hand shot is inserted on two further occasions. Then she passes a tramp asleep on the pavement and his outstretched hand reminds her of the killing. She starts back and there is a scream on the soundtrack, coinciding with a cut to Crewe's studio and a shot of the landlady discovering his body. The scream in fact belongs to the landlady and, according to Barry Salt, this is the first example in film history of the shock cut – 'a cut to a different scene accompanied by a sharp discontinuity in the accompanying sound.'[92] The landlady telephones the police.

At this point Frank re-emerges, as one of the team on the case. At Crewe's studio, he starts to look for clues, his survey of the room echoing Alice's experiences on the previous evening. Frank glances out of the window, looks at the jester painting, at the frothy dress, and finally at the nude sketch. He then discovers a glove on the floor, but as he is about to show it to the officer in charge the camera tracks forward very quickly to reveal to Frank the identity of the corpse. This revelation is accompanied by his realisation that the glove belongs to Alice, and their trivial conversation about it earlier falls adroitly into place as a way of planting information later to be mobilised by the narrative. Frank now chokes back this information, and the jester shot is used again to provide an ironic commentary upon his plight. As Lindsay Anderson suggested, 'The malevolently smiling jester is used as a sort of dumb commentator on the story.'[93]

Alice meanwhile returns home, rushes to her bedroom and climbs into bed still dressed as her mother is about to wake her with a cup of tea. A brief shot, which again divides the screen space into two, shows Alice to the right of frame rushing up the stairs while her mother appears on the left with the cup of tea; a succinct demonstration that suspense does not require montage but can be generated within the integral space of a single shot. Once in the bedroom, Alice's mother removes the cover from the birdcage and the bird's song fills the room. Drawing attention to the presence of sound in this way was a common ploy in early sound film, although the more usual device involved the opening of windows or doors to let sound in. Alice dresses hurriedly, still in a daze, and Hitchcock reverts to the montage style of earlier sequences by cutting in shots of Frank's photograph on the bedroom wall. Alice's agitated state of mind is again constructed through a series of telling 'reminder' images. And the bird's singing seems unnaturally amplified, adding to the scene's expressionist quality.

And so to the celebrated 'knife' sequence. Alice comes downstairs and goes into the shop/living room. She goes into the phone booth to telephone Frank. As in the bird song scene, the opening and closing of the booth door enables a play with the soundtrack, eliminating most of the ambient sound when Alice shuts the door and reintroducing it as she emerges. She decides against phoning and is soon seated with her parents at the breakfast table. The room opens on to the shop, and one of the customers stands at the door talking about the killing. She complains about the 'unBritish' nature of stabbing and keeps using the word 'knife'. Gradually, the soundtrack is manipulated to eliminate all

The 'knife' sequence

words except 'knife', which resounds on the track, slightly louder with each repetition. Eventually Alice's father breaks in and asks her to cut some bread. Her hand moves tentatively towards the breadknife (similar to the one she plunged into Crewe) and, on the final distorted sound of 'knife' and in an involuntary reflex gesture, she flings the knife from the table.

The 'knife' episode is one of the most quoted sequences in film history, and it was the one that attracted the attention of the critics of the day. Hugh Castle, in *Close Up*, suggested that the sequence 'is about the only one which we have on record in which sound has been definitely instrumental in the development of the drama.'[94] The 'knife' sequence, with its expressionist manipulation of the soundtrack, seemed to demonstrate the possibilities of a departure from the 'photographs of people talking' that dialogue films seemed to invite. It also counterpoints sound and image, with the woman's dialogue from off-screen space matched to a big close-up of Alice. Counterpointing sound and image, instead of synchronising them, was favoured as the artistic path for the sound picture by the film intellectuals of the day. It was a way of overcoming the sound recorder's 'misleading faculty of being able to record the actual', to borrow Paul Rotha's famous formulation.

The 'sound counterpoint' position had been given a considerable boost by the publication in *Close Up* in 1928 of the manifesto on sound film written by Eisenstein, Pudovkin and Alexandrov, which argued that the 'first experimental work with sound must be directed along the lines of its distinct non-synchronisation with the visual images.'[95] It went on to discuss the techniques of counterpointing sound and image and argued against the simple use of sound to achieve 'photographed performances of a theatrical sort'. Hitchcock's aural experiments in *Blackmail*, the 'knife' sequence in particular, seem to belong in spirit with the avant-garde thinking of the Soviet film-makers. The statement was published in English in October 1928, a few months before Hitchcock actually started on the production of *Blackmail*. This is not to suggest that Hitchcock had read Eisenstein before making the film, but that his thinking and that of avant-garde artists such as Eisenstein were not so far apart when it came to reflecting on the art of cinema. Indeed, as Rachael Low was later to suggest:

At a time when the whole cinema world was uncertain, most film makers fumbling, the critics theorising and the Soviet film makers as yet lacking the resources to put their ideas into practice, it was this shrewd and practical professional who unhesitatingly showed how sound could be made an integral part of film technique.[96]

The 'knife' sequence, which is relatively brief, condenses Alice's traumatised state in a particularly effective manner which is reinforced soon after by the prolonged and intensified 'twang' of the shop doorbell ringing to announce another customer. Again the sound is distorted by being amplified and placed on a close-up of Alice registering her agitation. The 'knife' sequence is also marked by a fluid use of camera movement and an intricate cutting pattern which produces the terminal shock effect when the knife flies out of Alice's hand. The scene opens with a full 'theatrical' shot, with the *mise en scène* organised in depth and all the characters in view. The gossiping woman is in the background, with Alice's family seated round the table in the foreground. She begins her 'knife' patter and there is a cut to a medium close shot of Alice. The camera then pans somewhat unsteadily from Alice to the gossip, then back to Alice. A closer shot of Alice follows, and with the word 'knife' beginning to dominate the soundtrack, the camera tilts slightly to the breadboard as she reaches for the knife. The close shot of her hand holding the knife is held, and on the final, much amplified 'knife' there is a cut back to the original full shot.

The construction of the scene in terms of Alice's subjective perceptions on the soundtrack – the distortion of the dialogue – has been accompanied by a subjectivising in the camera placement and movement. This part of the scene begins and ends on what might be termed an objective third-person view of the event, with all the participants in view and the camera placed in the optimum viewing position in respect of clarity of exposition. However, the cutting isolates Alice in close shots and further removes her from her surroundings by shadowing out the background. The camera moves between her and the gossip and back again, emphasising the particular impact of the comments on Alice herself, and the return to 'objectivity' occurs at the point when she is jolted out of her nightmare reverie. Alice then goes back into the shop to serve a customer, but when she comes back to the breakfast table there is a return to subjectivity in a close shot of her with the background shadowed out again and the piercing 'twang' of the shop doorbell.

The new customer is Frank, fresh from the murder scene and of course aware of Alice's implication in the killing of Crewe. His visit to the shop, on the pretext of using the telephone, is actually to see Alice and to sort out the mess she is in. The conflict between love and duty which Hitchcock cited as the plot basis for the film begins in earnest here, with Frank realising the truth but wanting to talk to Alice before he does anything about it. Indeed, his action in secreting the discovered glove from his colleagues has already tipped the balance towards love. A brief shot shows a man outside the shop, who then comes in and breaks up the fraught conversation between Frank and Alice in the telephone booth. This man, Tracy, is the shadowy figure from earlier, the man who was lurking outside Crewe's apartment, who knows about Alice's role in the killing and has discovered her other glove at the scene of the crime. Now he holds her fate in his hands, and there follows a cat and mouse game, primarily between the two men although Alice is the one really threatened at this point. The tension is played out initially in the public context of the shop, with several interruptions – the presence of Alice's father, a customer entering, a boy delivering newspaper billboards, one of which bears the ominous message 'Chelsea murder'. Tracy orders a cigar and manoeuvres Frank into paying for it. He then invites himself to breakfast, and proceeds to discuss the situation with Frank whilst tucking into bacon and eggs. At this point, Tracy is toying with Frank and Alice and savouring his power over them.

The narrative then cuts to police headquarters, where Crewe's landlady is being questioned about the murder. The shift in narrative space is by way of a shot of the malevolently smiling jester, whose presence previously had been a mocking warning to both Alice and Frank and whose presence now constitutes a threat to Tracy. The woman identifies him from the book of 'mug' shots and the inspector orders him to be picked up. We return to the family sitting room via a shot of the inspector sitting in front of the jester painting which dissolves into a shot of Tracy in his chair striking an identical pose.

A phone call warns Frank that the police are on their way to arrest Tracy. The scene contains brief snatches of apparently inconsequential dialogue – 'Hello', 'Yes', 'What?', 'Who?' – before Frank closes the telephone booth door and the soundtrack fades to an inaudible mumble. Alice's father is in the shop, a cut to him at the counter indicating a frustrated listener. However, as spectators we have been supplied with enough information to make sense of the scene and to understand the confident way in which Frank returns to Tracy and Alice. Hitchcock achieves this through allusion, leaving the spectator to infer meaning from the minimal sights and (especially) sounds. 'What?' and 'Who?' acquire almost immediate meaning in the context of the narrative flow.

The telephone call shifts the balance of power to Frank, and he begins to toy with Tracy. Alice, caught between two posturing males, is mesmerised and in a way a spectator despite being at the centre of the 'game'. The camera moves between the two men as the balance of power switches from one to the other. Alice is occasionally caught in

The ominous newspaper billboard

the middle, the camera moving from the men to catch her in close-up as her fate is decided against an image of her agonised face. As in the 'knife' sequence, key dialogue is delivered by a character not visible to the audience whilst the camera searches out its impact upon the heroine. Indeed, although the 'knife' sequence represents the most dramatic example of the counterpointing of sound and image, Hitchcock uses it at several points in the film.

The police arrive and Tracy attempts escape by leaping through a window. He is pursued by Frank and other policemen and the film moves into the final sequence, designed to reprise the opening. It begins with the shot of the spinning hub cap which opened the film and then repeats some of the other shots of the police wagon speeding through the streets. These are intercut with shots of Tracy in a taxi which eventually arrives at the British Museum, where he disembarks with the police hot on his heels. As we have seen, the Schüfftan process enabled Hitchcock to situate the denouement in a dramatic and familiar public place, a strategy which anticipates the use of locales such as the Statue of Liberty (*Saboteur*), London's Royal Albert Hall (both versions of *The Man Who Knew Too Much*), San Francisco's Golden Gate Bridge (*Vertigo*), and Mount Rushmore (*North by Northwest*). Tracy runs through the cavernous interior of the museum, climbs down a rope near a massive Egyptian sculpture, runs through the Reading Room, and eventually ends up on top of the building, on the dome. Trapped, he is about to accuse Alice when he crashes through the glass dome. The impact is conveyed mainly through the soundtrack. We hear the crash, see the shattered glass and, after a few seconds' delay, hear the sound of the body landing hundreds of feet below.

At various points in the pursuit (on nine occasions, to be precise), the film cuts to inserts of Alice sitting at a table staring into space, ostensibly mesmerised by events. The final shot in the sequence shows that in fact she has been writing a note to Frank to tell him that she intends to admit to the killing. The alternating montage works in an ironic way, and at the climax of the pursuit which conveniently masks Alice's involvement she goes off to Scotland Yard to confess. One part of the sequence – the pursuit – works to protect her, whilst the other moves her towards an admission of guilt.

At this point the film is still on course to satisfy Hitchcock's

The chase at the British Museum

original conception of the resolution – and it could have ended with a repetition of the opening, with Frank arresting Alice and putting her through the same procedures of arrest and interrogation that we saw at the beginning. Alice goes to see the Inspector and Frank is present in the room. She is about to say that it was she who killed Crewe when the telephone rings and the Inspector asks Frank to deal with her. They move into the corridor, where Alice confesses her 'crime' but explains that she was defending herself. They arrive at the entrance and, as at the beginning, a joke is shared with the policeman on the door about 'lady detectives' taking over Frank's job. But as the three of them are laughing, the camera moves towards them and Alice is isolated in a close shot reluctantly mouthing laughter. Her gaze shifts from the men and is directed off-screen. There is a cut to the jester image, as yet unlocated in the diegetic space although strongly signalled by Alice's off-screen glance.

As before, this shot functions symbolically, commenting on Alice's plight. There is a cut back to Alice, then a return to the jester shot. This time, however, the image is located and we see the painting being carried from the entrance hall, away from the camera. This is the final shot: we watch as the painting is carried into the recesses of the police station. Throughout, the soundtrack has been filled with the laughter of the men, counterpointed with Alice's retreat into silence. An ambiguous, and for *Blackmail* perhaps an appropriate, last conjunction of image and sound.

A LANDMARK FILM
. . . .

Despite Paul Rotha's contemporary verdict that the film would be 'completely forgotten in a few months', *Blackmail* has proved to be a film with a sustained presence in criticism. This is partly a function of the interest in Hitchcock from the perspective of authorship, a key early work adumbrating the Hitchcockian world and relating clearly to a number of later Hitchcock classics. Yet *Blackmail* is much more than an apprentice piece, a sketch for the mature American films. It is a key film in cinema history.

For most critics, it is the ear-catching 'knife' sequence which marks the film out. But its status as a landmark film depends on much more than this particular innovation, striking though it must have been to audiences barely used to the talkies. As Elisabeth Weis has demonstrated, many sequences in the film indicate a film-maker unwilling to submit to the quickly established 'rules' of dialogue shooting.[97] Films of the period were expected to show the source of dialogue, but Hitchcock frequently has the sound source in off-screen space, as in the mumbled exchanges between Crewe and Tracy outside the artist's apartment or in the 'knife' sequence itself. Although parts of the film, such as the Lyons Corner House sequence, are photographed predominantly in long master shots to avoid the cutting of the image which might have posed problems for the cutting of the soundtrack, such sequences are atypical. In fact, Hitchcock gave himself greater licence in the cutting by utilising off-screen sound so frequently. He also often moves both camera and actors, despite the problems of cumbersome pre-positioned microphones and the soundproofed camera booth. A good example of this is the potentially static sequence in which Alice, Frank and Tracy discuss the implications of their situation before the police arrive. The camera shifts constantly, isolating the actors in turn and allowing the sound to interact dramatically with the images.

Blackmail has many qualities. It is a traditional film in so far as it provides a summary of conventional silent film style and narration; it is revolutionary, in its bold use of the novel techniques of sound; it is modern in its self-consciously 'artistic' mode of narration; and it is post-modern in its eclectic stylistic character. As well as being a key film in the history of sound pictures, it is also a landmark film in cinema generally. Unlike some other classic films, however, *Blackmail* seems infinitely adaptable to the shifting currents of critical study. The director himself spoke of another of his films as 'a fascinating design', adding that 'One could study it forever.' He might have been speaking of *Blackmail*.

NOTES

·························

1 *Kine Weekly*, 4 July 1929, p. 53.
2 S. Eyüboglu, 'The authorial text and postmodernism: Hitchcock's *Blackmail*', *Screen*, vol. 32 no. 1, Spring 1991.
3 *The Bioscope*, 26 June 1929, p. 31.
4 *Daily Mail*, 24 June 1929.
5 *Close Up*, August 1929, p. 133.
6 Charles Barr, 'Blackmail: Silent and Sound', *Sight and Sound*, Spring 1983, p. 123.
7 Other examples would be *The Birth of a Nation* (long narrative film structure), *Battleship Potemkin* (montage), *The Jazz Singer* (sound), *Citizen Kane* (deep focus cinematography).
8 Elisabeth Weis, *The Silent Scream* (Rutherford, NJ: Fairleigh Dickinson University Press, 1982), pp. 30–1.
9 Eric Rohmer and Claude Chabrol, *Hitchcock* (New York: Frederick Ungar, 1979); D. Linderman, 'The Screen in Hitchcock's *Blackmail*', *Wide Angle*, vol. 4 no. 1, 1980; Tania Modleski, *The Women Who Knew Too Much* (London: Methuen, 1988); William Rothman, *Hitchcock – The Murderous Gaze* (Cambridge, Mass.: Harvard University Press, 1982).
10 See R. Mottram, 'American Sound Films, 1926–1930', in Elizabeth Weis and John Belton (eds.), *Film Sound* (New York: Columbia University Press, 1985).
11 Statistics based on Harry Geduld, *The Birth of the Talkies* (Bloomington: Indiana University Press, 1974), Appendix B, p. 274.
12 See Barry Salt, *Film Style and Technology* (London: Starword, 1983), chapter 12.
13 *Sight and Sound*, Summer 1949, p. 94.
14 *Kine Weekly*, 1 September 1927.
15 Rachael Low, *The History of the British Film 1918–1929* (London: Allen & Unwin, 1971), p. 204.
16 Douglas Gomery, 'Economic Struggle and Hollywood Imperialism: Europe Converts to Sound', *Yale French Studies*, no. 60, 1980, p. 82.
17 Quoted in Lotte Eisner, *Murnau* (London: Secker & Warburg, 1973), p. 85.
18 François Truffaut, *Hitchcock* (London: Paladin, 1986).

19 *Kine Weekly*, 2 August 1929, p. 29.
20 *Kine Weekly*, 4 April 1929.
21 Michael Balcon, *A Lifetime of Films* (London: Hutchinson, 1969), p. 34.
22 *Kine Weekly*, 5 July 1928, p. 21.
23 *Kine Weekly*, 25 April 1929, p. 21.
24 *Kine Weekly*, 6 December 1928, p. 20.
25 *Kine Weekly*, 23 May 1929, p. 21.
26 *The Bioscope*, 1 May 1929, p. 20.
27 *The Bioscope*, 8 May 1929.
28 *The Bioscope*, 10 July 1929, p. 20.
29 *Kine Weekly*, 8 November 1928.
30 *Kine Weekly*, 4 April 1929, p. 38.
31 Low, *The History of the British Film 1918–1929*, p. 204.
32 *Kine Weekly*, 14 June 1928, p. 33.
33 *Kine Weekly*, 12 July 1928, p. 27.
34 *Kine Weekly*, 2 August 1928, p. 31.
35 *The Bioscope*, 9 January 1929, p. 24.
36 *Kine Weekly*, 21 February 1929.
37 *The Bioscope*, 3 April 1929, p. 21.
38 *Kine Weekly*, 2 August 1928, p. 31.
39 *Kine Weekly*, 27 June 1929, p. 30.
40 *Kine Weekly*, 3 January 1929, p. 95.
41 *Kine Weekly*, 24 January 1929, p. 33.
42 *Kine Weekly*, 28 March 1929, p. 25.
43 *The Bioscope*, 10 April 1929, p. 25.
44 Ibid.
45 Details of the temporary studios are in *Kine Weekly*, 28 March 1929, p. 25; *The Bioscope*, 10 April 1929; and P. Warren, *Elstree: The British Hollywood* (London: Elm Tree Books, 1983), p. 43.
46 *Kine Weekly*, 16 May 1929, p. 35.
47 *Downhill* (Novello, 1927), *Easy Virtue* (Coward, 1927), *Juno and the Paycock* (O'Casey, 1930), *The Skin Game* (Galsworthy, 1931).
48 Michael Powell, *A Life in Movies* (London: Heinemann, 1986), pp. 191–3.
49 Film of a voice test for the actress is held in the National Film Archive, London. See also Donald Spoto, *The Life of Alfred Hitchcock* (London: Collins, 1983), p. 118.
50 *Kine Weekly*, 3 January 1929, p. 95.
51 Rodney Acland, *The Celluloid Mistress* (London: Allan Wingate, 1954), p. 35.
52 Truffaut, *Hitchcock*, p. 78.

53 Barr, 'Blackmail: Silent and Sound', p. 123.

54 John Russell Taylor, *Hitch* (London: Faber & Faber, 1978), p. 101.

55 Low, *The History of the British Film 1918–1929*, p. 246.

56 Quotation from the *Daily Mail* incorporated in an advertisement for the film in *The Bioscope*, 6 October 1927.

57 *The Bioscope*, 26 June 1929.

58 *Variety*, 10 August 1929.

59 *Variety*, 9 October 1929.

60 *Kine Weekly*, 10 October 1929, p. 18.

61 See Taylor, *Hitch*, p. 82, and Spoto, *The Life of Alfred Hitchcock*, pp. 95, 123.

62 Spoto, *The Life of Alfred Hitchcock*, p. 123.

63 *Close Up*, August 1929, p. 135.

64 *Close Up*, October 1929, p. 257.

65 *Close Up*, January 1930, pp. 17–18.

66 Paul Rotha, *The Film Till Now* (London: Spring Books, 1967), pp. 405–6.

67 Ibid., p. 321.

68 Forsyth Hardy (ed.), *Grierson on Documentary* (London: Faber & Faber, 1966), p. 72.

69 Ibid., p. 74.

70 *The Film Society Programmes* (New York: Arno Press, 1972), p. 227.

71 Ibid., pp. 177–8.

72 *World Film News*, April 1937, p. 15. Also published in 1937 was a collection of articles, *Footnotes to the Film*, edited by Charles Davy, which included a piece by Hitchcock with comments on *Blackmail*.

73 *The Penguin Film Review*, no. 1, 1946, p. 23.

74 Ernest Lindgren, *The Art of the Film* (2nd edition, London: Allen & Unwin, 1963), p. 107.

75 Ibid., p. 147.

76 *Sequence*, no. 9, 1949. Reprinted in A. LaValley (ed.), *Focus on Hitchcock* (Prentice-Hall, 1972), p. 51.

77 Rohmer and Chabrol, *Hitchcock*, p. x.

78 Ibid., p. 152.

79 Ibid., pp. 22–3.

80 Robin Wood, *Hitchcock's Films* (London: Zwemmer, 1965), p. 29. See also Wood's later comments in *Hitchcock's Films Revisited* (New York: Columbia University Press, 1989), pp. 230–1.

81 Peter Wollen, 'Hitchcock's Vision', *Cinema* (UK), no. 3, 1969, p. 4.

82 Charles Barr (ed.), *All Our Yesterdays* (London: BFI, 1986), p. 20.

83 Modleski, *The Women Who Knew Too Much*, p. 30.

84 Hardy (ed.), *Grierson on Documentary*, p. 74.

85 Anderson in LaValley (ed.), *Focus on Hitchcock*, p. 49.

86 Raymond Durgnat, *The Strange Case of Alfred Hitchcock* (London: Faber & Faber, 1974), pp. 29–30.

87 *Kine Weekly*, 28 March 1929, p. 31.

88 Davy (ed.), *Footnotes to the Film*, article by Hitchcock, p. 3.

89 Ibid., pp. 3–4.

90 Hitchcock used this phrase dismissively in relation to early talkies. See Truffaut, *Hitchcock*, p. 73.

91 Lotte Eisner, *The Haunted Screen* (London: Secker & Warburg, 1973), pp. 119–27.

92 Salt, *Film Style and Technology*, p. 284.

93 In LaValley (ed.), *Focus on Hitchcock*, p. 51.

94 *Close Up*, vol. V no. 2, 1929, p. 135.

95 *Close Up*, vol. III no. 4, 1928, p. 10.

96 Low, *The History of the British Film 1918–1929*, p. 192.

97 Weis, *The Silent Scream*, pp. 30–1.

CREDITS

· ·

Blackmail

GB
1929
Production company
British International
Pictures Ltd.
UK trade show
21 June 1929
Director
Alfred Hitchcock
Assistant Director
Frank Mills
Dialogue
Benn W. Levy
Screenplay
Alfred Hitchcock from the
play by Charles Bennett
**Photography
(black and white)**
Jack Cox
Music
Campbell & Connelly
**Music compiled and
arranged by**
Hubert Bath
Harry Stafford
Music played by
British International
Symphony Orchestra,
conducted by John Reynders
Editor
Emile de Ruelle
Art director
Wilfred C. Arnold
Executive producer
John Maxwell
Additional sc
Garnett Weston
Charles Bennett
Camera assistant
Derick Williams
Clapper boy
Ronald Reame
Additional art direction
Norman Arnold

Stills
Michael Powell
Sound
Harold King
96 minutes
Silent version
6740 ft

Anny Ondra
Alice White
(Voice dubbed by Joan
Barry)
Sara Allgood
Mrs White
Charles Paton
Mr White
John Longden
Frank Webber
Donald Calthrop
Tracy
Cyril Ritchard
Artist
Hannah Jones
Landlady
Harvey Braban
Chief Inspector
Ex-Detective Sgt. Bishop
Detective-sergeant
Phyllis Monkman
Gossip
Percy Parsons
Crook
Johnny Butt
Sergeant
Alfred Hitchcock
Harassed Underground traveller

Note: The print in the
Treasures of the National
Film and Television
Archive's collection is of the
silent version. It is from this
version that the frame stills
are drawn.

BIBLIOGRAPHY

· ·

Alexander, R. *Blackmail* (Readers Library Publishing, 1929). Novelisation based on the Bennett play.

Anderson, Lindsay. 'Alfred Hitchcock', *Sequence*, no. 9, 1949, reprinted in A. LaValley (ed.), *Focus on Hitchcock*, Prentice-Hall, 1972.

Barr, Charles. 'Blackmail: Silent and Sound', *Sight and Sound*, Spring 1983.

Bennett, Charles. *Blackmail*, a Play in Three Acts (London: Rich and Cowan, 1934).

Durgnat, Raymond. *The Strange Case of Alfred Hitchcock* (London: Faber & Faber, 1974).

Eyüboglu, S. 'The authorial text and postmodernism: Hitchcock's *Blackmail*', *Screen*, vol. 32 no. 1, Spring 1991.

Hitchcock, Alfred. 'Direction', in C. Davy (ed.), *Footnotes to the Film* (London: Lovat Dickson, 1937).

Rohmer, Eric, and Chabrol, Claude. *Hitchcock* (New York: Frederick Ungar, 1979).

Tom Ryall, *Alfred Hitchcock and the British Cinema* (London: Croom Helm, 1986).

Spoto, Donald. *The Life of Alfred Hitchcock* (London: Collins, 1983).

Weis, Elisabeth. *The Silent Scream* (Rutherford, NJ: Fairleigh Dickinson University Press, 1982).

Wood, Robin. *Hitchcock's Films Revisited* (New York: Columbia University Press, 1989).

Yacowar, Maurice. *Hitchcock's British Films* (Archon Books, 1977).

**BFI Film Classics '. . . could scarcely be improved upon . . .
informative, intelligent, jargon-free companions.'**
The Observer

Each book in the BFI Film Classics series honours a great film from the history
of world cinema – *Singin' in the Rain, Citizen Kane, Brief Encounter, Les enfants
du paradis*. With four new titles published each spring and autumn, the series is
rapidly building into a collection representing some of the best writing on film.

If you would like to receive further information about future BFI Film
Classics or about other books on film, media and popular culture from BFI
Publishing, please fill in your name and address and return the card to the BFI*.

No stamp is needed if posted in the UK, Channel Islands, or Isle of Man.

NAME

ADDRESS

POSTCODE

*North America: Please return your card to;
Indiana University Press, Attn: LPB, 601 N Morton Street, Bloomington, IN 47401-3797

**BFI Publishing
21 Stephen Street
FREEPOST 7
LONDON
W1E 4AN**